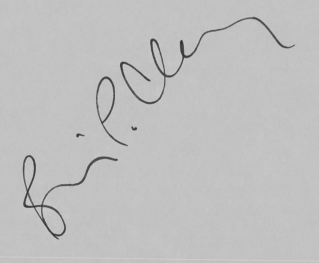

I and You and and Don't Forget Who

What Is a Pronoun?

To my sister Maggie, who is very much a word person.
—B.P.C.

To Wendy
—B.G.

Pronoun:
A word that takes the place of a noun.

NOTE: Some of the pronouns in this book are not printed in color. As each kind of pronoun is discussed, color type highlights only the corresponding pronouns. Can you find all of the pronouns?

I and You and and Don't Forget Who

What Is a Pronoun?

by Brian P. Cleary

illustrated by Brian Gable

CAROLRHODA BOOKS, INC. / MINNEAPOLIS

Pronouns can save us
a boatload of words
and help to avoid repetition.

They stand in for "Venice," "Marie," or "Spaghetti,"

because that's their specified mission.

Without **them** we'd say,
"Anne's father surprised Anne
and bought Anne
a sporty new truck.

Anne got so excited

that when Anne first saw it,

Anne couldn't believe
Anne's good luck."

Now, Anne is a really big
fan of her name,

but even she'd have to agree.

These phrases could sure use a "her" here and there,

and perhaps an occasional "she."

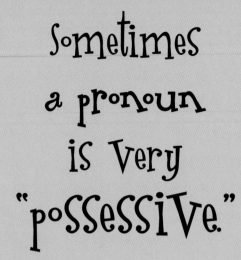

Nothing and all
are indefinite, too.

So are anyone,
no one, or any.

If it helps form a question, it's called "interrogative"— a very inquisitive pronoun.

What are you looking at?
Who is your daddy?

Which road do we take
to the hoedown?

So like a pinch hitter
Or a good baby-sitter,

the pronoun will say,
"You can go noun!
I've got your job covered."

Do you know?

ABOUT THE AUTHOR & ILLUSTRATOR

BRIAN P. CLEARY is the author of the Words Are Categorical series, including A Mink, a Fink, a Skating Rink: What Is a Noun? and Hairy, Scary, Ordinary: What Is an Adjective? He lives in Cleveland, Ohio.

BRIAN GABLE is the illustrator of Dearly, Nearly, Insincerely: What Is an Adverb? and Under, Over, By the Clover: What Is a Preposition? He lives in Toronto, Ontario, with his wife and two children.

Text copyright © 2004 by Brian P. Cleary
Illustrations copyright © 2004 by Brian Gable

Carolrhoda Books, Inc.,
A division of Lerner Publishing Group
241 First Avenue North
Minneapolis, MN 55401 U.S.A.

Website address: www.lernerbooks.com

Library of Congress Cataloging-in-Publication Data

Cleary, Brian P., 1959—
    I and you and don't forget who : what is a pronoun? / by Brian P. Cleary;
illustrations by Brian Gable.
        p.   cm. — (Words are categorical)
    Summary: Rhyming text and illustrations of comical cats present numerous
examples of pronouns and their functions, from "he" and "she" to "anyone,"
"neither," and "which."
    ISBN: 1-57505-596-1 (lib. bdg. : alk. paper)
    1. English language—Pronoun—Juvenile literature. [1. English language—
Pronoun.] I. Gable, Brian, 1949— ill. II. Title. III. Series.
PE1261.C58 2004
    428.2—dc21   2003001712

Manufactured in the United States of America
1 2 3 4 5 6 — JR — 09 08 07 06 05 04